LIGHT IN HOURS OF DARKNESS

Readings for the grief-stricken selected and arranged by

DOROTHY MASON FULLER

● ABINGDON PRESS

● NASHVILLE   ● NEW YORK

LIGHT IN HOURS OF DARKNESS

Copyright © 1971 by Abingdon Press

All rights in this book are reserved.
No part of the book may be reproduced in any
manner whatsoever without written permission of
the publishers except brief quotations embodied in
critical articles or reviews. For information address
Abingdon Press, Nashville, Tennessee.

ISBN 0-687-22013-0
Library of Congress Catalog Card Number: 77-162456

Excerpts from *Kontakion For You Departed* by Alan Paton, copyright © 1969 by Alan Paton. Used by permission of Jonathan Cape, Limited, publisher.

Selections abridged from "A Word from Frances" by Frances Gunther, in *Death Be Not Proud* by John Gunther, Copyright © 1949 by John Gunther. Reprinted by permission of Harper & Row, Publishers, Inc.

The quotation from *Beyond Our Selves* by Catherine Marshall, copyright © 1961 by Catherine Marshall, and the quotation from *To Live Again* by Catherine Marshall, copyright © 1957 by Catherine Marshall, are used with permission of McGraw-Hill Book Company.

The selection by Kim Malthe-Bruun, Copyright © 1955 by Random House, Inc., from *Heroic Heart* by Kim Malthe-Bruun, translated by Gerry Bothmer, reprinted by permission of the publisher.

The selections by Alfred Schmidt-Sas and Heinrich von Lehndorff-Steinort, Copyright © 1956 by Pantheon Books, Inc., a division of Random House, Inc., from *Dying We Live,* edited by Gollwitzer, Kuhn and Schneider, reprinted by permission of the publisher

Excerpts are reprinted by permission of Charles Scribner's Sons from *For You Departed,* pages 18-19 and 156, by Alan Paton, Copyright © 1969 Alan Paton; and from *The New Being,* pages 149 and 172-74, by Paul Tillich, Copyright © 1955 Paul Tillich.

An excerpt is reprinted from *Witness to the Truth* by Edith Hamilton by permission of W. W. Norton & Company, Inc. Copyright © 1948, 1957 by W. W. Norton & Company, Inc.

SET UP, PRINTED, AND BOUND BY
THE PARTHENON PRESS, AT NASHVILLE,
TENNESSEE, UNITED STATES OF AMERICA

To God the Holy Spirit
from whom we came, by whom we live, to whom we go
I dedicate with love and gratitude
this small book
which his inspiration in a dark hour first proposed
and which his patient guidance
brought at last to completion
after he had delivered me out of trouble
and led me into abundant life

INTRODUCTION

Every century differs from those that have gone before. Every culture develops, according to its own ideals and values, customs that mold and set its people apart.

Every human being is unique. Yet, in one respect, all who have ever lived are akin. Trained and disciplined by parents and teachers in childhood, we must all contend with difficulty and pain and sorrow as adults, and we must all die.

As Edith Hamilton has observed, "Our problem, the universal problem each one upon the earth must solve, is how to live." Uncertain of our way, sensing our mortal weakness, we long for light, strength, wisdom to guide us. In every age there have been those who found them. In every civilization there have been men who triumphed over disasters. Today they speak to you and me, beset as they were. Anxiety, suffering, and grief, they tell us, can be transcended. Many have found an angel in the clouds, light at the heart of darkness. We are not alone.

"Be not afraid." You are more than flesh and blood. Your spirit, offered to the all-powerful, deathless Spirit of Life to fulfill its purpose—the purpose for which you were created—will become invincible if you but trust it. Your deepest needs are God's loving concern. Take heart, then, in trouble and learn how true is his promise: "My grace is sufficient for thee: for my strength is made perfect in weakness."

Death is only a horizon;
and a horizon is nothing save the limit of our sight.

—Rossiter W. Raymond

SORROW STUNS AND BEWILDERS

Sorrow—unpredictable, mysterious, cruel—crashes into our lives, leaving us stunned and bewildered. We slowly recover a sense of reality only to find that we have lost—and it would seem for always—the taste for life, the joy and exhilaration of life, the passion and ambition of life, even perhaps the love of life and the will to live!

What shall we do with this dreadful thing so unexpected, so unwelcome? It dogs us; it will not let us alone; it invades our sleepless hours; it lies, a crushing weight, on our hearts during the days that seem endless. We resent it, we rebel against it, we cry out in our agony—but there seems no relief.

—V. B. Demarest

Cast all thy care on God. . . . Never brood over thyself; never stop short in thyself; but cast thy whole self, even this very care which distresses thee, upon God. Be not anxious about little things; . . . commit thy daily cares and anxieties to Him, and He will strengthen thy faith for any greater trials. Rather give thy whole self into God's hands, and so trust Him to take care of thee in all lesser things, as being His, for His own sake, whose thou art.

—E. B. Pusey

NOTHING TO LIVE FOR?

The first moment of personal heartbreak seems too terrible to be borne. Grief envelops, utter lostness is in the heart, wild questions are upon the lips. Why is this sorrow mine? Why do the innocent suffer? Why must the good and beautiful be senselessly hurt? Why are those so needed taken from us? . . .

At this point there seems nothing to live for. The world is dissolved about us and we grope blindly for a way. We move forward day by day, how, we do not know. Naught but God's grace saves us until we learn to forgive ourselves. This is what someone wise calls the first creative act of "grief's slow wisdom." We face our limitations and understand with complete surety that everything we long for of endurance or peace or happiness comes to us only through his touch upon our souls.

—CARMEN HEATH BLANC

In love's service only the wounded may serve.

—THORNTON WILDER

I am with thee to deliver thee. —JEREMIAH 1:8

YOUR DEFENDER IS WITHIN

Thy sorrows will seem to thee insuperable, and thine afflictions past the power of comfort. . . .

But if thou, O blessed soul, shouldest know how much thou art beloved and defended by that Divine Lord, in the midst of thy loving torments, thou wouldest find them so sweet that it would be necessary that God should work a miracle to let thee live. . . .

He is within that fighteth for thee, and He is strength itself.

—Miguel de Molinos, 1640-1697

Your bereavement admits you to one of the great fellowships in the world—that fellowship of those who have suffered. Nothing which one can say or do can help in the hour of grief as much to bring comfort as the companionship of one who, also, has passed through the valley of the shadow of death.

—Author Unknown

SORROW IS A LONELY ROAD

There are experiences into which you have to go all by yourself. With the best will in the world, even your dearest friends can't go all the way with you; always there must be closed doors around the innermost citadel of the soul.

This happens in sorrow. Our best friends can go part of the way along that road with us, and how much it means to us to have their companionship! But there is a point beyond which they cannot accompany us, and beyond that is the real stab and ache of sorrow. . . . When such experiences come . . . it makes all the difference in the world to be sure of Jesus Christ, and the blessed assurance only He can bring us of the presence and power of God in all the experiences of life. . . . He was upheld by the confidence that God, His heavenly Father, was with Him, even along the loneliest stretches of the way. . . .

The same life-changing Friendship is available for you and me. . . .

If you have to face a sorrow which sunders you from your dearest friends, you can share it with God, and His friendship will enable you to see beyond all that baffles, and could embitter you. You do not have to be alone: God in Christ can walk that road with you, to the very end.

—A. E. GOULD

A HUSBAND LOOKS BACK

Writing of the terminal illness of his wife soon after her death, a modern-day English writer observed:

It is incredible how much happiness, even how much gaiety, we sometimes had together after all hope was gone. How long, how tranquilly, how nourishingly, we talked together that last night!

And yet not quite together. . . . You can't really share someone else's weakness, or fear or pain. . . .

We both knew this. . . . The end of hers would be the coming of age of mine. We were setting out on different roads. This cold truth, this terrible traffic regulation ("You, Madam, to the right—you, Sir, to the left") is just the beginning of the separation that is death itself.

—C. S. Lewis

Grief is inconsolable in that the gap made can never be filled with anyone else than the beloved. I stand near enough to the grave to know the cruelty of the gulf that separates, but the realization does not weaken faith.

—Charles H. Brent

MYRRH IS ALWAYS BITTER

Now consider first the myrrh. It is bitter; and this is a type of the bitterness which must be tasted before a man can find God, when he first turns from the world to God, and all his likings and desires have to be utterly changed. . . .

But there is yet another myrrh which far surpasses the first. This is the myrrh which God gives us in the cup of trouble and sorrow, of whatever kind it may be, outward or inward. Ah, if thou couldst but receive this myrrh as from its true source, and drink it with the same love with which God puts it to thy lips, what blessedness would it work in thee! . . . Yes, the very least and the very greatest sorrows that God ever suffers to befall thee proceed from the depths of His unspeakable love; and such great love were better for thee than the highest and best gifts . . . that He has given thee or ever could give thee, if thou couldst but see it in this light.

—Johannes Tauler, 1290-1361

The chief pang of most troubles is not so much the actual suffering, as our own spirit of resistance to it.

—Jean Nicolas Grou, 1730-1803

GRIEF MUST NOT BE REPRESSED

The grief that death brings is, of course, not all of one level. The death of an aged, helpless parent can be welcomed as a blessed release for the person whose work is finished. . . . When a younger person is known to be incurably ill in mind or body, one can mourn his passing without wanting his bondage to earth to be prolonged. Every death brings the sadness of separation to those who love. But it is when death comes prematurely, or violently, or suddenly and without warning, that the shock of bereavement can be life's bitterest experience. . . .

First, one must accept the inevitable. . . . The person who was a warm, sweet, living presence is no longer here, and will not be again except in memory. . . .

One must not expect all at once to adjust to it. It is part of "grief's slow wisdom" that only time can heal the poignancy of the hurt. To try to hurry the process is not so much disrespect toward the deceased as the creation of new inner conflicts in the living.

One must give expression without shame to his grief. . . . Repression can work serious havoc by driving the poison of sorrow inward.

—Georgia Harkness

SORROW BECOMES FRUITFUL FOR GOOD

Sorrow may be either a curse or a blessing, either without use and significance or a treasure of infinite worth. Jealously hidden in the heart, it blights all it touches . . . or it becomes completely worthless. . . . But when consecrated to God and to humanity, sorrow becomes fruitful for good in one's own life and pregnant with power to bless, heal, comfort, and cheer other lives.

To you who grieve let it be said that your sorrow is your own. You can keep it if you wish, but if you do so it will eat away your heart. Why not yield your sorrow to God? In every great grief there is an inner shrine that is yours alone; none can enter it but the divine Sufferer himself, and even he cannot do so without your invitation. Dear wounded one, open the door to him and let the quickening breath of his Spirit pass through that secret, lonely, desolate place. . . . Do not close your shrinking heart to him—let him in! His presence . . . will bring the peace of surrender, and then he will be able to heal the wounds which could not bear the touch of any other hand.

—V. B. Demarest

MISFORTUNE CANNOT HURT THE REAL SELF

Death is more the beginning of victory than the triumph of tragedy.

—Charles H. Brent

I never go to a funeral without thinking of this miracle of transformation which brings the bird out of the egg, the flower out of the seed, the dragon-fly out of its water lava. In his own mysterious way God has emptied the nest by the hatching method, and all that was excellent, lovable and permanent in the one we loved has found itself in the realm for which it was fitted. The body is only the empty shell, the shattered seed, the old husk, which the forces of nature will slowly turn back again into its original elements, to use over again for its myriad processes of building.

—Rufus Jones

No losses or misfortunes, whether public or private, can hurt the hidden man of the heart, our real self; still less can they impair that welfare of the universal life in which our little lives are included. The real or spiritual world is a kingdom of values, and all that is valuable in the eyes of the creator is safe forever more. Nothing that has real existence can ever perish.

—Plotinus, 205-290

LOVE HOLDS GRIEF AT BAY

It was my wish to stand with David and Jonathan outside the church after the service, to meet those who wished to speak to us. This is a sound and proper wish . . . for the comfort of it is quite immeasurable. It was an experience like no other in my life, and the memory of it is as intense as the memory of that far-off day when I first embraced you. My sister Dorrie wrote . . . that the church was filled with love. . . . Outside the church it enveloped us, filling me with such a pride that grief—visible grief—was held at bay. The Archbishop had said that for you it must have been a triumphant passing as you went forth to join that band of those who have fought the good fight and have finished the course and have kept the faith and have won the peace.

. . . And what made it triumphant was that you, in this country of fear and division, were loved by so many people of so many kinds and conditions. And this love included me also—it was our work and our home and our peace—and pride and thankfulness kept grief in its place.

—Alan Paton

GRIEVE WITHOUT GUILT

His body was all but gone and his head was a skull, with the fine sweet skin drawn tight over bones. All the lesser qualities, good, bad, and petty, had been drawn out of his face.

Staring at him I said, "I've teased you since the first about not really being handsome, and I still don't think you really were. But you are now. I've never seen anything as beautiful as your head right now."

"Ah," he said, "you know how to make a man feel good."

I had betrayed him and us by my behaviour, and he had betrayed us, too, by his irrational violence toward me, when it had seemed for a year afterwards that we should have to settle for so much less than the intense hopes . . . of our beginning.

He made a gesture as if to take that old guilt in his hands and break it over his knee. He wiped out all guilt including my nagging sense that I had made him, an orderly perfectionist, a most sloppy and clumsy wife.

"Yes, you've clumsy hands," he said, "and all that. But do you know, now, watching you try not to be messy, I find your messiness—endearing.
And do you know that taking care of me, doing these things you've had to do, you've never hurt me? . . ." He had time and perception, outside of any framework of confession, punishment, and absolution, to leave me free of guilt or regret toward him, for anything done or undone: to leave me grief without guilt.

It is this I should like to say, offering it with humility as wisdom, to everyone who loses someone he has loved and, inevitably, done less well by than he would like to have done: The dead don't, can't want guilt or regret.

—Lael T. Wertenbaker

THE WAY OF DELIVERANCE

Crisis brings us face to face with our own inadequacy and our own inadequacy in turn leads us to the inexhaustible sufficiency of God. This is the power of helplessness, a principle written into the fabric of life.

—Catherine Marshall

Often when the heart is torn with sorrow, spiritually we wander like a traveler lost in a deep wood. We grow frightened, lose all sense of direction, batter ourselves against trees and rocks in our attempt to find a path. All the while there is a path—a path of faith—that leads straight out of the dense tangle of our difficulties into the open road we are seeking. Let us not weep for those who have gone away when their lives were at full bloom and beauty. . . . Who shall say whether those who die in the splendor of their prime are not fortunate to have known no abatement, no dulling of the flame by ash, no slow fading of life's perfect flower.

—Helen Keller

A SORROWING MOTHER SPEAKS

Concerning the death of her adolescent son whose great promise was cut short by a brain tumor, John Gunther's wife wrote in a postscript to his book Death Be Not Proud:

Death always brings one suddenly face to face with life. Nothing, not even the birth of one's child, brings one so close to life as his death.

The impending death . . . raises many questions in one's mind and heart and soul. . . . What is the meaning of life? What are the relations between things: life and death? the individual and the family? the family and society? marriage and divorce? the individual and the state? medicine and research? science and politics and religion? man, men, and God?

All these questions came up in one way or another, and Johnny and I talked about them, in one way or another, as he was dying for fifteen months. He wasn't just dying, of course. He was living and dying and being reborn all at the same time each day. How we loved each day! "It's been another wonderful day, Mother!" he'd say as I knelt to kiss him goodnight.

I have always prayed to God, and talked things over with Him . . . when perplexed, or very sad, or also very happy. During Johnny's long illness, I prayed continually to God, naturally. God was always there. He sat beside us during the doctors' consultations, as we waited the long vigils outside the operating room, . . . as we agonized when hope ebbed away, and the doctors confessed there was no longer anything they could do. . . .

Life is a myriad series of mutations, chemical, physical, spiritual. That same infinitely intricate, yet profoundly simple law of life that produced Johnny . . . destroyed him. . . .

A single cell, mutating experimentally, killed him. But the law of mutation in its various forms is the law of the universe. It is impersonal, inevitable. Grief cannot be concerned with it. At least mine could not.

My grief, I find, is not desolation or rebellion at universal law or deity. I find grief to be much simpler and sadder. . . .

All the things he loved tear at my heart because he is no longer here on earth to enjoy them.

—Frances Gunther

WORTHY LIVES HONOR THE DEAD

Dr. Pember, an Englishman mourning the loss of a fine son, received the following letter:

I know very well there is no escape from grief. We cannot love very much without suffering much, and the very pain of our suffering is an evidence of the strength of our love, so that we cannot ever wish grief to be less than it is and must be. The best I can wish for you is that you may have courage and strength; you will yourself know where to seek and find it. Some of it you will get, I hope, from the pleasure you have had in Edward's life, and of his fine example. We who are left have to make our lives continue to be worthy of those from whom we are separated.

—Lord Grey, 1862-1933

DEATH BRINGS DEPTH TO LIFE

When Dean Inge was reflecting about the death of his twelve-year-old daughter, he wrote, "Bereavement is the deepest initiation into the understanding of the mystery of human life, an initiation even more profound than mutual human love." . . . We tend . . . to think that we have found the meaning of life when we are able to love and be loved. He says, No. It is when we love, and then that love is broken. . . .

It is the same thing that is meant by a young mother whose two-year-old daughter died when she says: "After that first ache and pain and emptiness, suddenly one day my life descended onto another level, and my heart keeps singing all the time."

The best hope any of us can have for people who have been bereaved in the most intimate, personal sense of love that is broken by death is that they may know something of a new depth and perspective to their lives and may have been introduced into a more profound understanding of the mystery of human life. Death brings depth to life.

—JOHN B. COBURN

Adversity, . . . far from being a mere nuisance or cruelty, is one of the constituent elements in all great living. When you and I have faced a personal calamity and have handled it well, we have added a new dimension to our character.

—HARRY EMERSON FOSDICK

BE OF GOOD COURAGE!

In thee, O Lord, do I put my trust: let me never be ashamed: deliver me in thy righteousness. Bow down thine ear to me; deliver me speedily: be thou my strong rock, for an house of defence to save me.
For thou art my rock and my fortress; therefore for thy name's sake lead me and guide me.

—Psalm 31:1-3

The angel of the Lord encampeth round about them that fear him, and delivereth them.
O taste and see that the Lord is good: blessed is the man that trusteth in him.

—Psalm 34:7-8

Be of good courage and he shall strengthen your heart, all ye that hope in the Lord.

—Psalm 31:24

The Lord is my strength and my shield; my heart trusted in him, and I am helped: therefore my heart greatly rejoiceth; and with my song will I praise him.

—Psalm 28:7

A HUSBAND'S CRY

Suppose that the earthly lives she and I shared for a few years are in reality only the basis for, or prelude to, or earthly appearance of, two unimaginable, super cosmic, eternal somethings. Those somethings could be pictured as spheres or globes. Where the plane of Nature cuts through them—that is, in earthly life—they appear as two circles. . . . Two circles that touched. But those two circles, above all the point at which they touched, are the very thing I am mourning for, homesick for, famished for. You tell me she goes on? But my heart and body are crying out, come back, come back. Be a circle, touching my circle on the plane of Nature. But I know this is impossible. I know that the thing I want is exactly the thing I can never get. . . . On any view whatever, to say "H. is dead" is to say "All that is gone." It is part of the past. And the past is the past and that is what time means, and time itself is one more name for death, and Heaven itself is a state where "the former things have passed away."

—C. S. Lewis

Shortly after his own wife had died, the general of the Salvation Army sent this message to one of his officers just bereft:

"Two words will signify the chief source of your consolation in the future: one will be *faith* and the other *work*. What those words signify has been my help, indeed has saved me from desolation, if not actual despair."

—William Booth

TO A BEREAVED HUSBAND

The following letter was written to Neville Talbot after his wife's death:

Your wife and mine were somewhat alike, I think, in character and nature, and they have both gone ahead of us, leaving us with two young children. . . . Possibly some of the things I learned then may be of use to you. . . . The letters that came in were, most of them, not in full possession of the Christian hope in immortality. I was profoundly grateful for the kindness in them, but sometimes they depressed me. . . . I knew that Nellie was alive, and that she was near me, and that she had attained real life at last, come to her own true existence, and that if I was thinking and loving worthily there ought to be a great gladness and thankfulness for her sake, and that I ought to fight down my own sorrows and fears, just exactly as I should fight down temptations of the lower order. I read the Gospels again to try to catch their spirit. . . . Two sayings struck, "If ye loved Me ye would rejoice because I go unto the Father," and "He is not the God of the dead, but of the living." All through I found this last the chief help when the disintegrating sorrow came back. It would not do to grudge her deliverance and gladness, who never grudged anything for me.

—DAVID CAIRNS

ACCEPT AND START AGAIN

Misfortune cannot be conquered by furious and continuing resentment. It can be conquered only by quiet acquiescence. We win victory over bereavement only when we face our loss, accept our loss, and then make our way through and beyond our loss. . . . We do so by deliberately re-entering the world of daily activity—the busy world of problems, duties, friendships, opportunities, satisfactions. An immolated, resentful, self-pitying life is a doomed life. Only the life which deliberately picks up and starts again is victorious.

—JAMES GORDON GILKEY

TURNING SUFFERING TO GOOD

Sorrowing for the loss of her son, a mother wrote of her own struggle to adjust, and the insights that followed:

Missing him now, I am haunted by my own shortcomings, how often I failed him. I think every parent must have a sense of failure, even of sin, merely in remaining alive after the death of a child. One feels . . . that one should somehow have found the way to give one's life to save his life. . . .

I wish we had loved Johnny more when he was alive. Loving Johnny more . . . What can it mean now? . . . To me it means loving life more, being aware of life, of one's fellow human beings, of the earth.

It means obliterating . . . the ideas of evil and hate and the enemy, and transmuting them, with the alchemy of suffering, into ideas . . . of charity.

It means caring more and more about other people, at home and abroad, all over the earth. It means caring more about God.

I hope we can love Johnny more and more till we, too, die and leave behind us, as he did, the love of love, the love of life.

—Frances Gunther

BEREAVEMENT IS A PART OF LOVE

If, as I can't help suspecting, the dead also feel the pains of separation (and this may be one of their purgatorial sufferings), then for both lovers, and for all pairs of lovers without exception, bereavement is a universal and integral part of our experience of love. It follows marriage as normally as marriage follows courtship or as autumn follows summer. It is not a truncation of the process but one of its phases; not the interruption of the dance, but the next figure. We are "taken out of ourselves" by the loved one while she is here. Then comes the tragic figure of the dance in which we must learn to be still taken out of ourselves though the bodily presence is withdrawn, to love the very Her, and not fall back to loving our past, or our memory, or our sorrow, or our relief from sorrow, or our own love.

—C. S. Lewis

INSIGHT AFTER TRAGEDY

A fatal automobile accident took the life of Morgan Vining and seriously injured his wife. Afterward she wrote:

I had nine weeks in bed to contemplate the wreckage of my world. I realized then that beauty and courage and human love, though indispensable, were not enough. During a long winter I sought desperately for the rock of truth on which to build my life anew and found it in the silent worship of the Quaker meeting. In discovering there the love of God, I found the love of neighbor infinitely widened and deepened. . . . I have come to understand that we see only a small part of the whole pattern of existence. Sorrow and suffering give opportunities for growth. Disappointment often opens doors to wider fields. The tragedy of death, as someone wiser than I has said, is separation, but even separation may not be permanent. . . . Often it seems that those who have most to give the world are the very ones . . . taken from it in the flower of their youth and vigor. It is hard to understand why this should be so, unless—and this I believe to be true—they have done whatever it was they had to do here, have fulfilled their secret contract with this world, and have been released for more important work elsewhere.

—Elizabeth Gray Vining

GRIEF TURNS US TO GOD

For some of us it takes grief and pain to turn us to our Lord. Sorrow brings us to the end of our resources and then we turn to him who has constantly sought us. Given such a world as ours, death can no more be left out than birth; and given love, we are inevitably bound to grief. . . .

Love and sorrow are all of a piece, just as much of a whole as day and night. . . . Sorrow that is pent up, deadened with opiates or driven into the unconscious will be slow to heal. Let us weep and we shall be comforted in the derivative sense of the word: God will bulwark us with fortitude, with strength, to bear the death of a beloved.

—Josephine Moffett Benton

CHRIST CAN TRANSFIGURE SORROW

Jesus in his life and teaching did not set himself to give a verbal explanation of this world's inescapable paradox of sorrow and of seeming evil; but for himself and for others he made sorrow redeeming through his revelation of a spirit which could transfigure it with courage and steady it with trust, and that has been the effect of his spirit from that time until this. Whenever sad people think of him . . . they may not understand their sadness any better; but there is newness in the way they feel. Their iciness is melted; all that was hard and frozen turns into a stream of gentle emotion which waters in their souls a garden where the flowers of a fragrant peace begin to grow. They are not afraid of sadness now, for the love of God is walking by their side.

—WALTER RUSSELL BOWIE

God has a way of opening the eyes of those who suffer. To them are revealed the great secrets of his kingdom. Perhaps one of the great missions of your life from this hour, will be to help others to understand these secrets. You can be the means of bringing "light in the hour of darkness."

—AUTHOR UKNOWN

OFFER DEAR ONES BACK TO GOD

All love that binds and holds and coerces and refuses to let go destroys and consumes. A parent must set his child free; a couple must be free to choose to love each other every day till death parts them. When death comes, let them go.

It might be helpful to think of this as an offering. They have been given to us—free gifts: love, husbands, wives, children, colleagues, fellow workers, members of a common life. As they have been given to us, let us offer them back.... If we are Christians we offer them back to God....

Each successive bereavement can bring greater gentleness, less passion to possess things or prestige or power, an abiding courage, a grounding in life unseen and eternal that cannot be shaken, a willingness not to have your own way all the time, a sense . . . that pain somehow brings greater power than even knowledge, a realization that the deepest satisfactions are in a peace and joy that the world can neither give nor take away, that all life finally is grace.

—John B. Coburn

SORROW MUST BE LIVED WITH

Sorrow cannot be fought and overcome; it cannot be evaded or escaped; it must be lived with. . . . We must learn how to shoulder the burden of it, to carry it so that it does not break our stride or sap the strength of those about us through their pity for our woe. Death of the young and vigorous when they still have much to experience and much to give, loss of the rare and precious person in midstream, is comparatively unusual in good times, but in times of war it becomes tragically frequent. Somehow we must learn not only to meet it with courage, which is comparatively easy, but to bear it with serenity, which is more difficult, being not a single act but a way of living.

"Men help each other by their joy," Ruskin said, "not by their sorrow." Sorrow may be the plow and the harrow which dig the soil and crumble it fine, but it is the fresh-springing plant of joy that is directly of benefit to our fellows.

—Elizabeth Gray Vining

The deeper that sorrow carves into your being the more joy you can contain.

—Kahlil Gibran

ONE DAY AT A TIME

Some there are that torment themselves afresh with the memory of what is past; others, again, afflict themselves with the apprehension of evils to come; and very ridiculously both—for the one does not now concern us, and the other not yet. . . . One should count each day a separate life.

—Seneca, 4 b.c.-a.d. 65

Anyone can carry his burden, however hard, until nightfall. Anyone can do his work, however hard, for one day. Anyone can live sweetly, patiently, lovingly . . . till the sun goes down. And this is all that life really means.

—Robert Louis Stevenson, 1850-1894

Sufficient unto the day is the evil thereof. —Matthew 6:34

As thy days, so shall thy strength be. —Deuteronomy 33:25

I the Lord will hold thy right hand, saying unto thee, Fear not, I will help thee. —Isaiah 41:13

THIS DAY ONLY IS OURS

He that hath so many causes of joy . . . is very much in love with sorrow . . . who loses all these pleasures, and chooses to sit down upon his little handful of thorns. Enjoy the blessings of this day if God sends them; and the evils of it bear patiently and sweetly: for this day only is ours; we are dead to yesterday, and we are not yet born to the morrow.

—Jeremy Taylor, 1613-1667

To Fénelon in 1689 Madame Guyon wrote:

When the moment of duty and of action comes, you may be assured that God will not fail to bestow upon you those dispositions and qualifications which are appropriate to the situation in which His providence has placed you. Act always without regard to *self*. The less you have of self, the more you will have of God.

Later he wrote this affirmation which has helped many sorrowing people struggling to adjust to a changed way of life:

Cheered by the presence of God, I will do each moment, without anxiety, according to the strength which He shall give me, the work that His Providence assigns me.

—Fénelon, 1651-1715

I steer my bark with Hope ahead and Fear astern.

—Thomas Jefferson, 1743-1846

FRESH INSIGHT BRINGS HIGH RESOLVE

I wrote . . . that bereavement is not the truncation of married love but one of its regular phases—like the honeymoon. What we want is to live our marriage well and faithfully through that phase too. If it hurts (and it certainly will) we accept the pains as a necessary part of this phase. . . . We were one flesh. Now that it has been cut in two, we don't want to pretend that it is whole and complete. We will still be married, still in love. Therefore we shall still ache. But we are not at all—if we understand ourselves—seeking the aches for their own sake. The less of them the better, so long as the marriage is preserved. And the more joy there can be in the marriage between dead and living, the better. . . .

I will turn to her as often as possible in gladness. I will even salute her with a laugh. The less I mourn her the nearer I seem to her.

An admirable program. Unfortunately it can't be carried out. Tonight all the hells of young grief have opened again; the mad words, the bitter resentment, the fluttering in the stomach, the nightmare unreality, the wallowed-in tears. For in grief nothing "stays put." One keeps on emerging from a phase, but it always recurs. Round and round. Everything repeats. Am I going in circles or dare I hope I am on a spiral?

But if a spiral, am I going up or down it?

How often—will it be for always?—how often will the vast emptiness astonish me like a complete novelty and make me say, "I never realized my loss till this moment"! The same leg is cut off time after time. The first plunge of the knife into the flesh is felt again and again.

—C. S. Lewis

DEATH CANNOT KILL WHAT NEVER DIES

They that love beyond the World cannot be separated by it.

Death cannot kill what never dies.

Nor can Spirits be divided that love and live in the same Divine Principle; the Root and Record of their Friendship.

If Absence be not Death, neither is theirs.

Death is but Crossing the World, as Friends do the Seas; They live in one another still.

For they must needs be present, that love and live in that which is omnipresent.

In this Divine Glass, they see Face to Face; and their Converse is Free as well as Pure.

This is the Comfort of Friends, that though they may be said to Die, yet their Friendship and Society are . . . ever present, because Immortal.

—WILLIAM PENN, 1644-1718

Penn knew whereof he spoke. His beloved wife had died. . . . His mother . . . had died just on the eve of his great first voyage to Pennsylvania. His son, . . . the only really promising one among his disappointing children, had coughed his ardent young life away at twenty. After . . . he had come to terms with his sorrow, Penn wrote the lines quoted above. They embody . . . a calm and utter conviction that what he says is true. He *knows*.

—ELIZABETH GRAY VINING

THIS I BELIEVE

I am certain that the visible and invisible are all one *now*, aspects of the same inescapable existence and communion, though our very limited five senses can do little to inform us what is beyond their restricted range. I am certain that those who have passed beyond our sight are with us *now*, with no long waiting and no reality of separation. One day when this stage of our pilgrimage is over, we shall go to them. They already have come to us, and that, believe me, is no mere guesswork. It remains to us to be as worthy of them as we can, to cheer them by our faith and courage, if we may, and to keep ourselves steadfast . . . on that level of living where in a rarer atmosphere the clouds and shadows flee away.

—W. H. Elliott

There is no grief that time does not lessen and soften.

—Cicero, 106-43 b.c.

I DO NOT FEAR DEATH

On the eve of his execution in 1943 a victim of Nazism charges his wife and comforts her.

Let us be thankful for everything that we had in each other and with each other. For you, beloved, everything is of course much, much worse than for me. For my own person, you must feel assured, I do not fear death. I fear it only as it affects you and our beloved sweet children. . . .

One thing I ask of you. You will be very sad in the time about to come—that I know, yet I cannot avert it. I know that you will certainly not forget me. But when you speak of me, do it with cheerful manner. . . . I have lived my short life blithely (perhaps too blithely), and that is how I want to be remembered. . . .

Wherever I may be, I shall always pray for you. . . . You are the very dearest thing that I leave behind me on this earth. . . . Please, please, do not consume yourself with grief over my fate. . . . I have already told you: I have no fear, inwardly I have settled accounts with myself, I shall face everything proudly and with head erect, I shall entreat God not to withdraw his strength from me, and my last thought will be you and the children. . . .

We shall go on loving each other beyond death as dearly as we loved each other in life.

—HEINRICH VON LEHNDORFF-STEINORT

CONSOLATION FOR THE SORROWING

Death has no scissors to cut the cords of love.

—Peter Marshall

Those who die are, in respect of us, but as absent for a few years, it may be only months. Their seeming loss should tend to loosen our hold on the world, where we must lose everything, and draw us to that other world where we shall find all again.

— Fénelon

I have the quiet consolation, steadily growing, that death is only an incident, and that its power has been so broken that it can do little else than create a momentary break in intercommunication. Love somehow becomes more of a steady flame through death. If we hold in our inmost hearts those who have gone, and they in like manner hold us, death is already abolished.

—Charles H. Brent

THOU ART MY HELP

Show me thy ways, O Lord; teach me thy paths. Lead me in thy truth, and teach me: for thou art the God of my salvation; on thee do I wait all the day.

—Psalm 25:4-5

He healeth the broken in heart, and bindeth up their wounds.

—Psalm 147:3

There can hardly be any more potent cordial for fainting hearts or drooping spirits than a realization that, whatever we did for them on earth or left undone, we can help them now—by our kind and loving thoughts, most speedy of messengers, by our constant remembrance, by our prayers for them, by showing in ourselves that faith, that courage, that resolve which shall make them proud in so great a cloud of witnesses. That they help us, guide us, guard us—in the name of God, by the power of God, for the glory of God,—is, to some of us at least, a most vivid daily experience.

—W. H. Elliott

GOD WILL NOT FAIL YOU.

We shall steer safely through every storm, so long as our heart is right, our intention fervent, our courage steadfast, and our trust fixed on God. If at times we are somewhat stunned by the tempest, never fear. Let us take breath, and go on afresh.

—Francis de Sales, 1567-1622

I am poor and needy: make haste unto me, O God: thou art my help and my deliverer; O Lord, make no tarrying.

—Psalm 70:5

Why art thou cast down, O my soul? and why art thou disquieted within me? hope in God: for I shall yet praise him, who is the health of my countenance, and my God.

—Psalm 43:5

DEATH CANNOT DESTROY LOVE

Of course no one can help the suffering which comes in bereavement. Indeed, who would escape it if he could? It is the one means left to us by which to declare the reality and depth of our love for the one taken. Were there no pain it would mean there had been no love or too little love. Go on unanxiously with the glad knowledge that you and yours are tied by a bond against which death is as powerless as a cloud to extinguish the sun or a hammer to destroy a moonbeam.

—CHARLES H. BRENT

Those who are gone you love. Those who departed loving you love you still and you love them always. They are not really gone, those dear hearts and true; they are only gone into the next room, and you will get up presently and follow them, and yonder door will close upon you and you will be seen no more.

—WILLIAM MAKEPEACE THACKERAY, 1811-1863

LEARN FROM SORROW

The secret of finding joy after sorrow or through sorrow, lies, I think, in the way we meet sorrow itself. We cannot fight against it and overcome it. . . . We try to be stoical, to suppress our memories, to refuse to recognize the source of our pain, to kill it with strenuous activity. . . .

Or we try to escape from it through travel, books, entertainment or study. But when the trip is over, the book closed, the curtain lowered, the research accomplished, there is our sorrow waiting for us, disguised perhaps, but determined. . . .

What we must do, with God's help, is to accept sorrow as a friend, if possible; if not, as a companion with whom we will live for an indeterminate period; a companion of whom we shall always be aware but with whom we can work, from whom we can learn, and whose strength will become our strength. Together we create beauty from ashes, and find ourselves blessed in the process.

—Elizabeth Gray Vining

Truly my soul waiteth upon God: from him cometh my salvation. He only is my rock and my salvation; he is my defence; I shall not be greatly moved. . . .

My soul, wait thou only upon God; for my expectation is from him. He only is my rock and my salvation: he is my defence; I shall not be moved.

—Psalm 62:1-2, 5-6.

PRAY FOR LIGHT TO WALK BY

As soon as circumstances permit, grief must be sublimated into action. The worst thing a person can do is to withdraw into himself and brood. The best thing he can do is to carry on the work left unfinished, or do some useful work for others that otherwise would have been done in love for the person no longer present. . . .

There is no occasion in life when a person needs more to pray for God's sustaining strength, for light to walk by, for inner peace. . . . There is no reason why one should not pray for God's watchful care for the person now in God's nearer presence. . . .

Bereavement can be, not blankness and utter loss, but suffering that with all its poignancy is nevertheless the beginning of a richer fellowship with the Eternal. . . . If the bereaved person, alone with God, makes a new dedication of his life to God and his service, great peace and power can ensue.

—Georgia Harkness

All loving is a gift of grace from beyond ourselves. Christians, like infants, love because they were first loved.

—Sidney Callahan

LET GO! LET GOD!

To put God first in our lives, to love Him, trust Him, and obey Him, is to assure ourselves of joyous, fruitful living. It is to bring into our lives the fulfillment of this Bible promise: "The Lord shall guide thee continually."

—Author Unknown

Do everything for God, uniting yourself to Him by a mere upward glance, or by the overflowing of your heart towards Him. Never be in a hurry. . . . Do not lose your inward peace for anything whatsoever, even if your whole world seems upset. Commend all to God, and then lie still and be at rest. . . . Whatever happens, abide steadfast in a determination to cling simply to God, trusting to His eternal love for you; and if you find that you have wandered forth from this shelter, recall your heart quietly and simply.

—Francis de Sales, 1567-1622

CHRIST TEACHES MEN HOW TO LIVE

The Gospels are not an explanation or a theology. They are the record of a life. Men have asked of religion what religion does not give. You will ask it in vain for reasons and explanations, why this or that calamity has happened. Religion does not answer. It gives no reasons. It does not explain why. It shows men how. Our problem, the universal problem each one upon the earth must solve, is how to live. To that question the religion of Christ does give an answer, adequate for all needs and in all perplexities.

—Edith Hamilton

Every waking moment stand in God's presence with him in your heart. In quietness and confidence is your strength and from now on, when you go out . . . go as an ambassador of God, that through your abiding in him you may translate his words into daily living. . . . You can offer yourself as a living channel for him to pour through his healing wisdom; "I will not leave you comfortless, I will come to you." Accept this divine gift wholeheartedly.

—Letters of the Scattered Brotherhood

SEEK AND YE SHALL FIND

There is no getting over sorrow. I hate the idea. But there is a getting into sorrow and finding right in the heart of it the dearest of all human beings—The Man of Sorrows, a God. . . . I pray that you may never "get over" sorrow, but get through it, into it, into the very heart of God.

—Forbes Robinson

Learn that each day must be lived in My Power, and in the consciousness of My Presence, even if the thrill of Joy seems to be absent. Remember that if sometimes there seems to be a shadow on your lives—it is not the withdrawal of My Presence. . . .

Work in the calm certainty that I am with you.

—God Calling

To rest in the Lord does not mean sinking into the devotional cushion and putting the tail over the nose. It means the restful harmony of a ship that has found herself, in which all parts work together in perfect, selfless collaboration under the Captain's will.

—Evelyn Underhill

THE BEREAVED ARE NOT ALONE

We bereaved are not alone. . . . When it seems that our sorrow is too great to be borne, let us think of the great family of the heavy hearted into which our grief has given us entrance, and inevitably, we will feel about us their arms, their sympathy, their understanding.

Believe, when you are most unhappy, that there is something for you to do in the world. So long as you can sweeten another's pain, life is not in vain.

—HELEN KELLER

G.L.C., in a letter to a bereaved friend:

The way of acceptance brings you closer to Christ, and the meaning of His Cross. The way of acceptance brings you closer to Christ and the power of His resurrection. The living Christ is not apart from you. He is with you. He knows your grief and He shares it with you. The way of acceptance brings you closer to God because this one you love is with Him forever more. So may Christian joy dwell within you to make even good come from all this mystery of pain.

He that abideth in me, and I in him, . . . bringeth forth much fruit.

—JOHN 15:5

GRIEF CHANNELED INTO SERVICE

I was in the depths of grief, I might almost say of despair, for the light and sunshine of my house had been extinguished. . . . Mr. Cobden called upon me as his friend, and addressed me . . . with words of condolence. After a time . . . he said, "There are thousands of houses in England at this moment where wives, mothers and children are dying of hunger. "Now," he said, "when the first paroxysm of your grief is past, . . . come with me, and we will never rest till the Corn Law is repealed."

I accepted his invitation. . . . I felt in my conscience that there was a work which somebody must do . . . and from that time we never ceased to labor hard on behalf of the resolution. . . .

There were others before us; and we were joined. . . . by hundreds, and afterwards by thousands, and afterwards by countless multitudes; and afterwards famine itself, against which we had warred, joined us; a great minister was converted, and minorities became majorities, and finally the barrier was entirely thrown down. . . . Since then, though there has been suffering . . . yet no wife and no mother and no little child has been starved to death as the result of a famine made by law.

—JOHN BRIGHT, 1811-1889

COMFORTED—THAT WE MAY COMFORT

Blessed be . . . the God of all comfort; who comforteth us in all our tribulation, that we may be able to comfort them which are in any trouble, by the comfort wherewith we ourselves are comforted of God.—II Corinthians 1:3-4

The most important sphere of giving . . . is not that of material things, but lies in the specifically human realm. What does one person give to another? He gives of himself, of the most precious he has, he gives of his life. This does not necessarily mean that he sacrifices his life for the other—but that he gives him of that which is alive in him; he gives him of his joy, of his interest, of his understanding, of his knowledge, of his humor, of his sadness, of all expressions and manifestations of that which is alive in him.

—Erich Fromm

LOVE IS STRONGER THAN DEATH

Every death means parting, separation, isolation. . . . Our souls become poor and disintegrate insofar as we want to be alone, insofar as we bemoan our misfortunes, nurse our despair and enjoy our bitterness, and yet turn coldly away from the physical and spiritual need of others. Love overcomes separation and creates participation in which there is more than that which the individuals involved can bring to it. Love is the infinite which is given to the finite. Therefore we love in others, for we do not merely love others, but we love the Love that is in them and which is more than their or our love. . . . Of course, there is no love which does not want to make the other's need its own. But there is also no true help which does not spring from love and create love. . . . And the gratitude of those who receive help is first and always gratitude for love and only afterwards gratitude for help. Love, not help, is stronger than death. But there is no love which does not become help.

—Paul Tillich

That sense now called brotherhood—the vivid consciousness that God is present to us in the souls of our fellows—is the very essence of love.

—Evelyn Underhill

BE THE BEARER OF LOVE

Lord, make me an instrument of Thy peace.

—Saint Francis

Francis of Assisi no doubt often prayed for something for himself, or for the order he had founded, or for the chapel and huts at Porziuncola. But in his prayer he asks nothing for himself, or perhaps he asks everything, and that is that his whole life, all his gifts, his physical strength, shall be an instrument in God's hand.

And I say to myself, this is the only way in which a Christian can encounter . . . despair and sadness, and that is by throwing off his helplessness and allowing himself to be made the bearer of love, the pardoner, the bringer of hope, the comforter of those that grieve. And I believe that if you allow yourself to be so made, you will be so.

—Alan Paton

LET US HELP ONE ANOTHER

Life is short and we have never too much time for gladdening the hearts of those travelling the dark journey with us. Oh, be swift to love and make haste to be kind!

—Henri Frederic Amiel, 1821-1881

One of the great accompaniments of all the trouble and sorrow we experience is the sense of being knit into the life of our kind. So much more you must be feeling yourself a part of all whom you meet—a partaker in the loads which suffering humanity carries upon its shoulders. We must pay a great price for any knowledge we may acquire of life.

—Mabel Cratty

I'm going your way, so let us go hand in hand. You help me and I'll help you. We shall not be here very long, for soon death, the kind old nurse, will come back and rock us all to sleep. Let us help one another while we may.

—William Morris

THE BOND OF RELATEDNESS

The times of being fearful that we are lost in the . . . darkness, that we are forever caught in the briers . . . may serve to keep us humble. Alone we are indeed lost and our lives . . . without purpose; alone, we need to be members of one another. Empty, we need to be filled. Overcome with the darkness, we need to be carried into the Light of truth and the Warmth of love.

This we cannot do alone. . . . Loving our heavenly Father and his other children, we in time learn to be useful shepherds. . . .

As the hard shell of ego with its layers of apartness, indifference, pride, begins to be softened by the love of God and loving friends, the bond of relatedness with all mankind begins to grow. First to be felt may be a oneness with those who are hurt—whether in body, mind, or morals. . . .

Then there grows slowly . . . a realization that in being members of one another, not only are the weaknesses of mankind mine but also the strengths. . . .

All the gentleness of sweet friends, all the happiness of shining souls, . . . all the courage of those who have lived with fortitude, . . . all goodness is mine.

—Josephine Moffett Benton

JOY WITHIN SORROW IS POSSIBLE

Sorrow is the feeling that we are deprived of our central fulfillment, by being deprived of something that belongs to us and is necessary to our fulfillment. We may be deprived of relatives and friends nearest to us . . . which gave us a meaning of life, of our home, of honor, of love, of bodily or mental health. . . . All this brings sorrow in manifold forms, the sorrow of sadness, the sorrow of loneliness, the sorrow of depression. . . . But it is precisely this kind of situation in which Jesus tells his disciples that His joy shall be with them and that their joy shall be full. . . .

Jesus calls the poor, those who mourn, those who hunger and thirst . . . "blessed." And He says to them: "Rejoice and be glad!" Joy within sorrow is possible to those who are blessed. . . .

Jesus will give His joy to His disciples *now*. They shall get it after He has left them, which means in *this* life. . . .

Where there is joy, there is fulfillment. . . . In fulfillment and joy the inner aim of life, the meaning of creation, and the end of salvation, are attained.

—Paul Tillich

LOVE SURROUNDS OUR DEAD

Why do we claim that the world-beyond-death is a world without terrors? Because we believe that a God of love, unfailing and all-including love, planned this vast scheme-of-things. We cannot believe that He would frighten or hurt any of his children, either in life or after death. When terrifying things happen here on Earth they are (we believe) the work of something or someone other than our Father-in-Heaven. And the life-after-death? We believe that it is through a quiet door the dead pass, that it is in a friendly world they find themselves, that there they retain their identity and their love for us. At that point our speculations stop . . . but meantime our fear has faded. In place of dread a new quietness fills our hearts. We are confident that our dead are safe, and that around them as around us is a never-failing Divine Love.

—James Gordon Gilkey

"ASK, AND IT SHALL BE GIVEN YOU"

That suicide accounts for a dismaying number of deaths in our country and the rest of the world was merely a printed fact until our only son in his thirtieth year took that way out.

The plight of his lovely young wife compounded our sorrow. My personal grief was intensified because in an early period of unhappiness the same temptation had tormented me. It was then I first turned to God for help.

Light came. Life is ongoing, I was assured. To take my life would solve nothing, for beyond death I would have to learn the lesson assigned me here. What was I here for? Primarily to fulfill God's purpose; to grow in spiritual understanding and love. Every crisis, then, was a chance to prove that God's concern is our highest welfare and his power is unfailing. And so, in time, I came to trust life. A happy marriage, joyous motherhood, and satisfying years of community service ensued.

Then this dreadful tragedy. Why? I can only explain what happened next by saying that I flung myself into the arms of that trusted Presence who understood all.

Consoling insights followed. Death had only freed an immortal spirit from what was contrary to God's intent. Our son, though beyond our sight, was still within His care, and that promising life would be nurtured to its full stature, "strong in the Lord." I surrendered him to God's loving omnipotence.

Our son lives on in our hearts today, a vital, maturing spirit. We remember thankfully his gifts and the good times we had together. We speak freely of him to each other.

Such is not always the case. The mother of an adolescent suicide told me, "I envy you. I can never mention our boy.

It is too painful for my husband." How can one hope to become whole again if one locks away precious with painful memories?

To parents grieving for a suicide I offer this tested solace for despair. All over the world today are fathers and mothers mourning for the same reason you are. Pray for them, as for your needy self, that they may learn from this calamity all the good it has to teach. Ask God to comfort their hearts and forgive them any real or imagined part in the maladjustment of their child. This very hour you can take that first step toward peace and the healing of your own deep sorrow.

—S. T.

ZEST FOR LIFE RETURNS

Once before I wrote that my grief was done, and then it suddenly returned. . . . But now it will not return again. Something within me is waking from long sleep, and I want to live and move again. Some zest is returning to me, some immense gratefulness for those who love me, some strong wish to love them also. I am full of thanks for life. . . .

The book is done, too. . . . It has in some strange way refined some dross out of me. It has taught me . . . to accept the joys and vicissitudes of life, and to fall in love again with its strangeness and beauty and terror. . . .

I have made my song, alleluya. And may you rest where sorrow and pain are no more, neither sighing, but life everlasting.

—Alan Paton

WITH GOD IN INFINITE TIME AND SPACE

We must think of the dead as alive and joyful and we must rejoice in their happiness, remembering that we are in close and constant communion with them, our life only separated from theirs by the thinnest of veils. We must remember, too, that this does not separate us either from God—our eternal joy, who more than makes up all that we lack—or from the companionship of those who are with God in infinite time and space. Let us be brave and keep the eyes of our souls wide open to all these realities: let us see clearly around us those things which others only care to see dimly.

—Abbé de Tourville

MAN'S LINK WITH THE ETERNAL

There is in man, [Plato] holds, an inner center of reality which is inherently linked up with a divine and supersensuous world from which he has come and to which he indissolubly belongs. The supreme values of the deeper universe—beauty, truth, love and goodness—have their home and habitat in our souls as well as in the eternal nature of this deeper world of reality. We are in it and of it now and forever, for nothing physical and temporal can destroy that whose intrinsic nature is eternal. The soul that has become an organ of beauty, truth, love and goodness, which are eternal realities, is itself thereby an eternal and abiding reality and no longer doomed to the fate of things which belong to the world of time and space. . . .

Immortal life for Plato attaches essentially to the supreme spiritual values of life.

—Rufus M. Jones

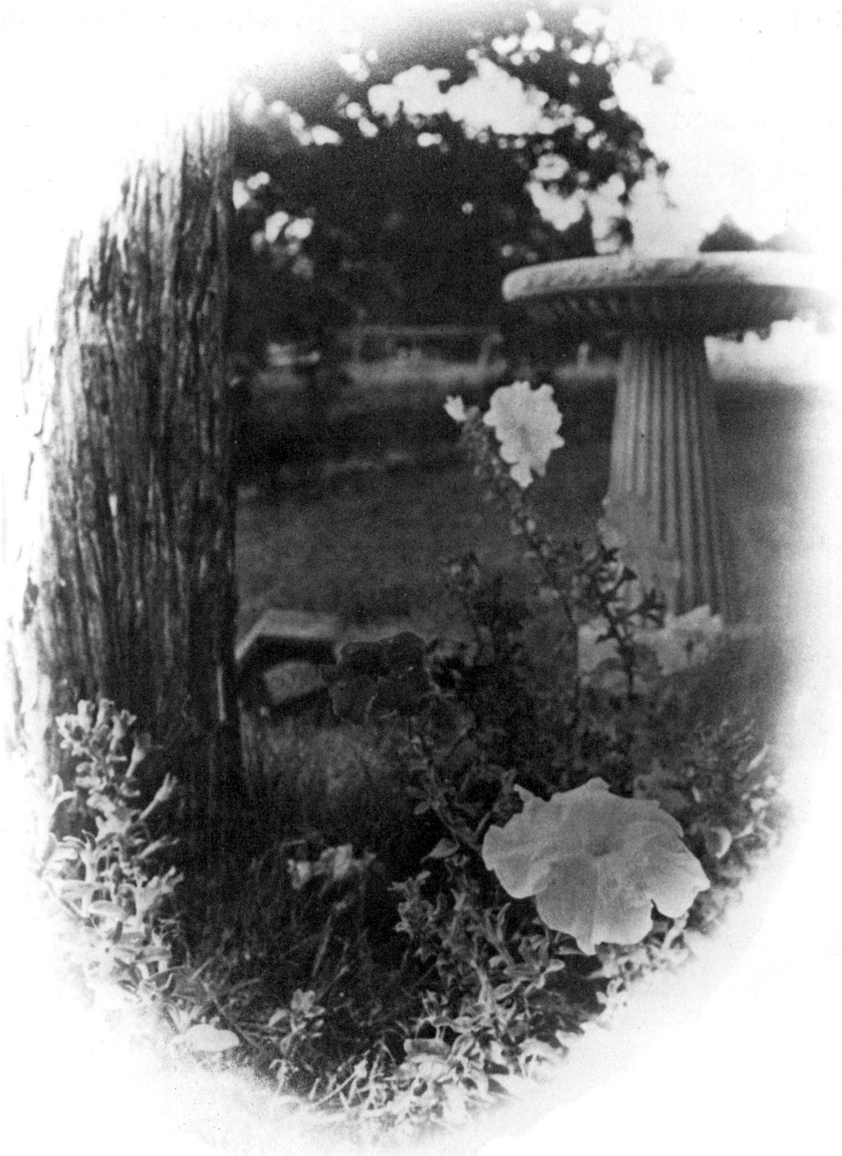

IF WE COULD ONLY KNOW

We are so apt to see only what souls go *from*. When our friend dies we think of all the warm delights of life, all the sweet friendships, all the interesting occupations, all the splendor of the sunlight. . . . If we could only know . . . the presence of God into which our friend enters on the other side, the higher standards, the larger fellowship with all his race, and the new assurance of personal immortality in God; if we could know all this, how our poor comfortless effort of comfort when our friends depart, our feeble raking over the ashes of memory, our desperate struggles to think that the inevitable must be all right; how this would all give way to something almost like a burst of triumph, as the soul we loved went forth to such vast enlargement, to such glorious consummation of its life!

—Phillips Brooks, 1835-1893

DEATH IS ENTRANCE INTO LIGHT

The faith of Christ is one that teaches more than a courage in face of death. The very character of death is transformed, replacing a gloomy prospect of loss and dissolution by a sense of liberated life. As we come to a more intimate experience of the reality of God we may enter into the overcoming power and strength of the great words of Christ: "I am the Resurrection and the Life." Death is swallowed up in victory, and, for those we love, is no longer a dark place of shadows but an entrance into the fuller light of God.

While it is natural that we should grieve at the withdrawal of loved friends from our physical sight, we may also rejoice in their new freedom and larger vision. We need to get away from the thought of the dead as lost to us and buried, and to realize them as having an ever vital part with us in the service of the Eternal.

—Christian Discipline, Part II, 1925

GIFTS OF LOVE

A sorrowing mother writes of love:

Love is always a costly thing. It asks much and we dare not refuse. Capacity for love determines capacity for pain. And the capacity for love of the most tender human heart compared to that of the heart of the Eternal is like the capacity of a cup in contrast with that of the ocean bed. God *is* love; his nature is love; the whole universe is a creation of his love and is bathed in the ocean of that love. . . .

If it cost him so much to give his own Son, and he gave him for me, would it be likely that unfeelingly he would take my child? No! No! If he loved us enough to give his Son, then God's dealings with us *must be the dealings of love, and the sorrows as well as the joys of our lives are the gifts of that love.*

—Author Unknown

Love all God's creation, the whole and every grain of sand in it. Love every leaf, every ray of God's light. Love the animals, love the plants, love everything. If you love everything you will perceive the divine mystery in things. Once you perceive it, you will begin to comprehend it better every day. And you will come at last to love the whole world with an all-embracing love.

—Fyodor Dostoevsky, 1821-1881

LOVE'S EVER-WIDENING CIRCLES

If we love God and give ourselves to Him, we must give ourselves to the whole world. . . .

One of the holy miracles of love is that once it is really started on its path, it cannot stop: it spreads and spreads in ever-widening circles till it embraces the whole world in God. We begin by loving those nearest to us, end by loving those who seem farthest. And as our love expands, so our whole personality will grow, slowly but truly. Every fresh soul we touch in love is going to teach us something fresh about God.

—Evelyn Underhill

YOURS, BUT NOT FOREVER

Kim Malthe-Bruun's farewell letter to his young sweetheart of twenty was written from Western Prison, German Section, Cell 411, April 4, 1945.

Lift up your head, you my heart's most precious core, lift up your head and look about you. . . . Live on now for the two of us. I am gone and far away and what remains is . . . a memory that should make you into a woman who is alive and warmhearted, mature and happy. You must not bury yourself in sorrow, for you would become arrested, sunk in a worship of me and yourself, and you would lose what I have loved most in you, your womanliness. Remember . . . that every sorrow turns into happiness—but very few people will in retrospect admit this to themselves. They wrap themselves in their sorrow, and habit leads them to believe that it continues to be sorrow. . . . The truth is that after sorrow comes a maturation, and after maturation comes fruit.

One of these days, Hanne, you will meet a man who will become your husband. Will the thought of me disturb you then? Will you perhaps then have a faint feeling that you are being disloyal to me or to what is pure and holy to you? Lift up your head, Hanne, lift up your head once again and look into my laughing blue eyes, and you will understand that the only way in which you can be disloyal to me would be in not completely following your natural instinct. You will see this man and you will let your heart go out to him—not to numb the pain, but because you love him with all your heart. You will become very, very happy because you will have found a soil in which feelings still unknown to you will come to rich growth. . . .

I should like to breathe into you all the life that is in me, so that thereby it could perpetuate itself and as little as possible of it be lost. That is willy-nilly what my nature demands.

Yours, but not forever,
KIM

A LITANY FOR THOSE WHO MOURN

Father of all mercy, we commit to thy loving care our dear ones, departed out of this world, and beseech thee to give us understanding and courageous hearts.

Loose us from the bitterness that casts a shadow over all the common day, that we may gain the peace which comes from ceasing to protest,

We beseech thee, good Lord.

For the years of fulfillment, for the joys we have known, and for the glad memories that crowd our hearts,

We thank thee, good Lord.

For the daily tasks which fill our empty hands, for habit born of years of training, which holds us steady in the storm,

We thank thee, good Lord.

For the unexpected tribute, and the revealing of new beauty in those we have known before; for eager hands held out to help us in our dire need, and for the understanding service of our friends,

We thank thee, good Lord.

For tears freely shed which heal and bring release, and which in thine own good time thou will wipe away,

We thank thee, good Lord.

For the strength, born of our own travail, to help others new in sorrow; for that rare insight vouchsafed us, which is the gift of grief,

We thank thee, good Lord.

For the ever present wounds of the spirit, which in God's mercy bring us near to Him, and by their very perpetuity prevent our leaving Him,

We thank thee, good Lord.

For the gradual but sure transformation of our physical loss into spiritual gain as the years go by,
We thank thee, good Lord.

For the courage which bids us carry on in new adventures, confident of the nearness and understanding of those we have lost,
We thank thee, good Lord.

For all those who share our precious memories, who knew and loved our dear ones and who now help to keep their memory clear,
We give thee special thanks, good Lord.

Above all, for the hope that thou hast given us through Thy Blessed Son Jesus Christ, of life eternal in the company of our loved ones,
We give thee grateful hearts, good Lord.

We thy servants who have passed through the valley of the shadow of death, fear no evil. Sanctify us through our grief, that we may know the close communion of the Saints, and lift our lives to theirs, and so live fully through the years. In the name of Him who was the firstfruits of them that sleep, Jesus Christ Our Lord. *Amen.*

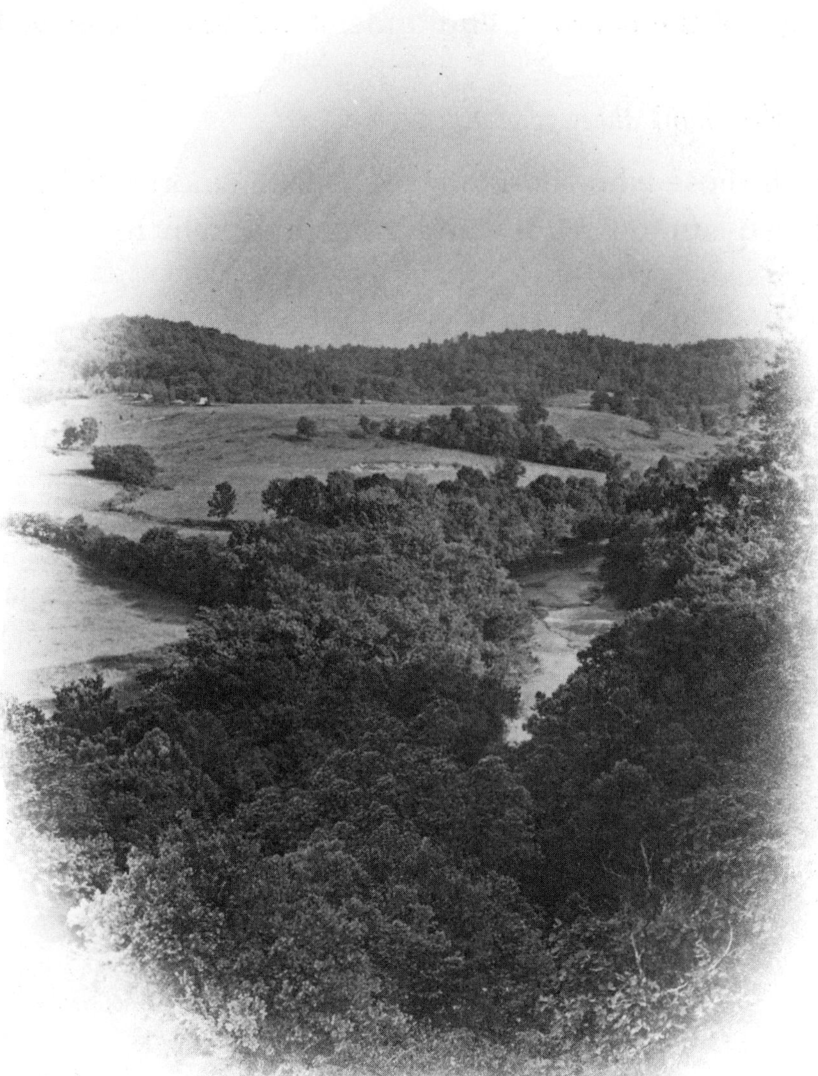

SURRENDER YOURSELF TO LIFE!

A brave man about to die addresses a loving plea to his wife:

In the measure in which I have become increasingly aware of your love, in the measure in which I have learned . . . to love you ever more deeply, in that measure the bright glow of kindness has spread wider, the confusion of the world has cleared away, strength and happiness have grown within me, and I have become well-disposed toward all men, . . . this, my dearest, has been your handiwork. And there was a merciful dispensation in your last visit, our last sense-perceptible union; had we known the future we might not have had strength enough. . . .

My plea is: Do not close yourself to the beauty of this world, surrender yourself to life, through your being, your art, through your voice, create joy, happiness, kindness, and peace. How much I should like to help you in that! Let all who have helped in shaping me know that these final hours and this death are the crowning of my life, and
that I remain completely yours

ALFRED SCHMIDT-SAS

ACKNOWLEDGMENTS

The compiler and publisher wish to express gratitude to the following individuals and publishers for permission to use copyrighted material:

Abingdon Press for excerpts from *Prayer and the Common Life* by Georgia Harkness.
Jonathan Cape Limited for excerpts from *For You Departed* by Alan Paton, copyright © 1969 by Alan Paton.
Peter Davies Limited for a passage by A. E. Gould from *Into the Valley* by A. E. Gould and V. Symonds, copyright 1964 by Peter Davies Limited.
de Koven Foundation, Tract Department, Sisters of Saint Mary for a *Litany for Those Who Mourn*, T-4.
Faber and Faber Limited for quotations from *A Grief Observed* by C. S. Lewis. Copyright © 1961 by C. S. Lewis. Reprinted by permission of Faber and Faber Limited.
Friends Journal for an excerpt from "Grief into Beauty" by Carmen Heath Blanc, which appeared in the March 1, 1963 issue.
Greenwood Press, Inc. for an excerpt from *The Life of John Bright* by G. M. Trevelyan, copyright © 1913 by Greenwood Press, Inc.
Harper & Row, Publishers, Inc. for material abridged from "A Word from Frances" by Frances Gunther, in *Death Be Not Proud* by John

Gunther. Copyright 1949 by John Gunther. Reprinted by permission of Harper & Row, Publishers, Inc.

London Yearly Meeting of the Religious Society of Friends for a passage from *Christian Discipline*, Part II—1925.

Longman Group Limited for an extract from the letter of Lord Grey to Dr. Pember in *Grey of Falloden* by G. M. Trevelyan.

An excerpt is reprinted from *Witness to the Truth* by Edith Hamilton by permission of W. W. Norton & Company, Inc. Copyright © 1948, 1957 by W. W. Norton & Company, Inc.

Pendle Hill Publications, Wallingford, Pennsylvania, for permission to quote from *The World in Tune* by Elizabeth Gray Vining.

Random House, Inc. for an excerpt from *Heroic Heart* by Kim Malthe-Bruun (Bothmer translation), copyright © 1953 by Random House, Inc.; for excerpts by Alfred Schmidt-Sas and Heinrich von Lehndorff-Steinort from *Dying We Live*, edited by Gollwitzer, Kuhn and Schneider, copyright © 1957 by Pantheon Books, Inc.

SCM Press Limited for part of a letter written by David Cairns in September 1921 to Neville Talbot on the death of his wife, from *David Cairns: An Autobiography*, SCM Press 1950.

Charles Scribner's Sons for excerpts reprinted by permission of Charles Scribner's Sons from *For You Departed*, pages 18-19 and 156, by Alan Paton. Copyright © 1969 Alan Paton; and from *The New Being*, pages 149 and 172-74, by Paul Tillich. Copyright © 1955 Paul Tillich.

The Seabury Press for selections from *A Grief Observed* by C. S. Lewis, copyright © 1961 by N. W. Clerk; and for an excerpt from *Instrument of Thy Peace* by Alan Paton, copyright © 1968 by Seabury Press, Inc.

United Church Press for excerpts from Josephine Moffett Benton, *Gift of a Golden String*. Copyright 1963 United Church Press. Used by permission.

Elizabeth Gray Vining for excerpts from "My World Was Wrecked Once," in *This I Believe*, © 1952 by HELP, Inc.; for an excerpt from *Shadow and Light in Bereavement*, published by the Representative Meeting, Religious Society of Friends, Philadelphia, 1959.

Lael Tucker Wertenbaker for an excerpt from *Death of a Man* by Lael T. Wertenbaker, © 1957, Random House.

The Westminster Press for quotations from *Twentieth-Century Spiritual Letters* by John B. Coburn. Copyright © 1967 The Westminster Press. Used by permission.

Zondervan Publishing House for excerpts from *Shade of His Hand* by V. B. Demarest.

Designer: Nancy Deyhle
Photographers: W. B. Witsell, Bracey Holt,
    Sid Dorris & Richard T. Lee
Type: 14 pt. Palatino, leaded 4 pts.*
Typesetter: Gulbenk
Manufacturer: Parthenon Press
Printing Process: Offset
Paper: Body: 70 lb. Bookcote
       Endsheets: 70 lb. Beckett Text
Binding: Kivar 5 Victoria

*(Others: Bembo Italic)